As surfers, we get a taste of nature from the front row whenever we paddle out – saltwater included! Something that stokes us most is watching wildlife at our usual surf spots or while exploring new waves far away. Pods of migrating whales pass through, only to return with calves by their sides months later. Sea lion pups swim among us. Seabirds and sea turtles make their homecomings to nest and lay eggs. Lizards and snakes soak up the warm sun alongside dusty trails.

Join us and our WiiLD crew of pals from around the world on the adventure of a lifetime!

Wishing you a WiiLDER Adventure,

Hubi & Luna

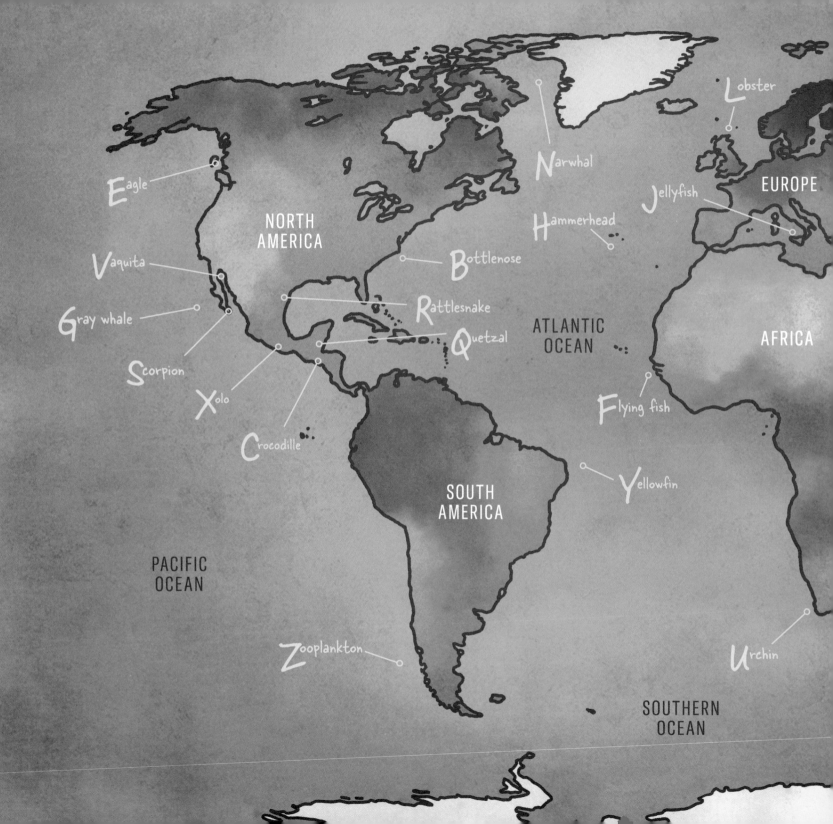

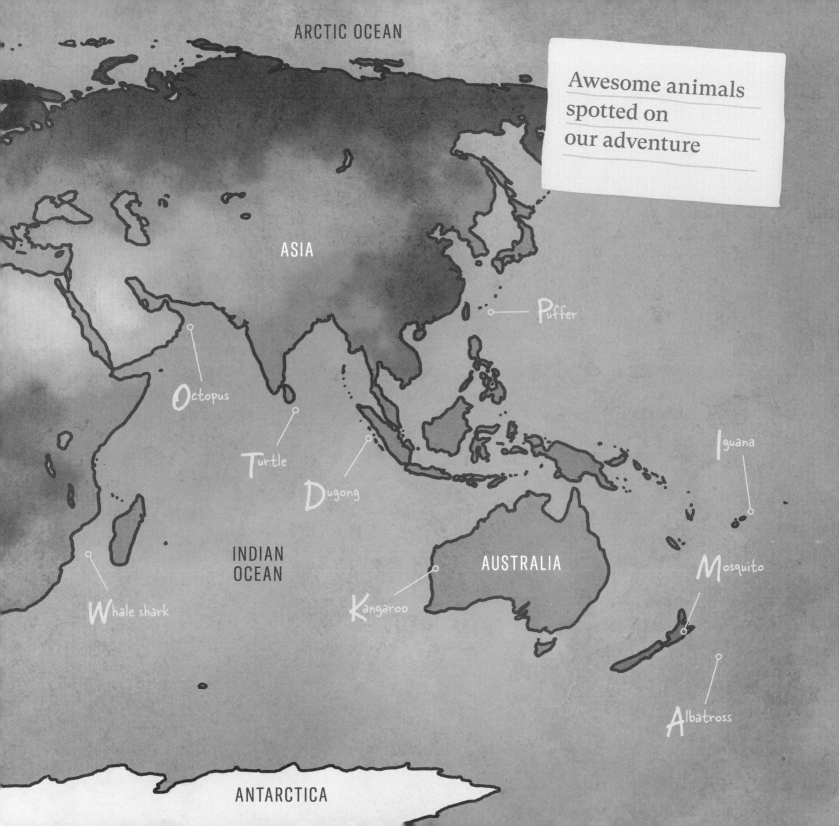

Off to explore our planet and oceans in search of surf and wildlife.

Hop aboard and meet some of the amazing creatures we cross paths with!

Albatross

Gliding above the ocean waves,
Far from shore for countless days.

The widest wings of any bird,
A life the beach gulls find absurd.

Many an ocean may you cross,
And wander like the albatross!

Wandering Albatross — Southern Ocean, New Zealand

Bottlenose

Dolphins love to chase their friends in games of tag.

What games do you like to play with your friends?

Bottlenoses live and play in groups,
Like packs of wolves or baboon troops.

Riding waves up and down the coast,
Is what these swimmers love the most.

What could make you feel more free,
Than surfin' with a dolphin or three?

Bottlenose Dolphin — Outer Banks, North Carolina, USA

Crocodile

Out where *El Rio* and the Pacific meet,
Are sharp-toothed dinos with scaly clawed feet.

For millions of years, crocs have survived,
By snapping up meals that walk or swim by!

American Crocodile – Guanacaste, Costa Rica

Dugong

Dugongs eat up to 90 pounds (40 kilos) of seagrass every day.

How many vegetables do you eat a day?

Like cows that graze in pastures all day,
Dugongs munch seagrass in warm shallow bays.

Swimming through the ocean ever so slow,
Feeding on the meadows waving below.

For this they've been called *cows of the seas*,
Just like their cute cousin, the manatee.

Dugong dugon — Mentawai Islands, Indonesia

Eagle

From a branch up high on an ancient tree,
A feathery hunter swoops swiftly to sea.

Without a splash, it plucks out a salmon,
And holds on tightly with each long, sharp talon.

Bald eagles rule Western Canada's skies,
Thanks to their speed and exceptional eyes.

Bald Eagle — Clayoquot Sound, British Columbia, Canada

Flying Fish

Have you ever seen a fish that flies?
A silvery swimmer that takes to the skies?

Launching from the ocean, gliding so fast,
Fleeing a tuna, hoping to last.

These winged fish are real – so small, sleek and brave,
Zipping through the air, above the warm waves.

Atlantic Flying Fish — Dakar, Senegal

Gray Whale

When they aren't singing to each other, whales breach and slap their tails to communicate.

How do you use your body to communicate?

When coldness returns and Alaskan days shorten,
Gray whales travel south to lagoons unforgotten.

We watch in awe as the grays spy-hop and breach,
While curling our toes on the warm desert beach.

Eastern Pacific Gray Whale – Laguna San Ignacio, Baja California, Mexico

Except for the "blind spot" in front of their noses, hammerheads can see all around.

How would you walk if you couldn't see in front of you?

Hammerhead

Where Atlantic volcanoes climb to the sky,
Gather wide-headed fish with far-spread eyes.

In the deep big blue, they loop in schools,
Groups of young hammerheads, so sleek and smooth.

With bulging eyes that can scan all about,
Except straight ahead, in front of their snout.

Smooth Hammerhead Shark — The Azores, Portugal

Iguana

In a Fijian forest by the sea,
Grows a lush and flowered hibiscus tree.

Upon its twisted trunk there stands,
A small iguana with blue and green bands.

A lizard we could watch for hours,
As it bobs its head and chomps on flowers.

Fijian Banded Iguana — Lau Islands, Fiji

Jellyfish

Our boat rolls gently on a summer night,
Under the stars, on a galaxy of light.

A swarm of jellies drifts in the sea,
Glowing purple for miles around Luna and me.

Glimmering creatures, pulsating jellies,
Tentacled drifters, nightlights of the seas.

Mauve Stinger Jellyfish — Sardinia, Italy

Kangaroo

On a dirt track down to Ningaloo,
We crossed a mob of kangaroos.

The marsupials stared and we did too,
With all of us wondering what to do.

After a minute and polite *g'day*,
We bid them *hooroo* as they hopped away.

Red Kangaroo — Ningaloo, Australia

Lobster

Lobsters spend their days in rocky caves.

Is there a cozy place where you like to hang out?

Lobsters gather in dark little caves,
To hide from predators on sunshiny days.

Lodged beneath ledges, spiny shell to shell,
Waving their antennae to feel and to smell.

But when the sun sets and night has fallen,
These critters come out for huntin' and crawlin'.

European Lobster — Northeast Scotland

Mosquito

A mosquito's wings beat up to 600 times per second.

How many times can you wave your arms up and down in 10 seconds?

A busy mosquito buzzes in the tent,
Drawn by our breath and tasty scent.

The wee blood sucker won't get another bite,
Not again, lil' mozzie, not once more tonight!

Corner to corner, my flashlight scans,
Then comes a tickle atop my hand.

So always remember to zip shut the screen,
For calm, cozy nights and mosquito-free dreams.

Saltpool Mosquito — Taranaki Peninsula, New Zealand

Narwhal

We're off exploring the high Arctic reaches,
Of Greenland's rocky fjords and odd sandy beaches.

What's this unique and beautiful creature?
A deep-diving whale with a unicorn feature!

As the pod of tusked narwhals plays in the sun,
We give up on surfing and admire their fun.

Narwhal — Baffin Bay, West Greenland

Octopus

A mollusk so clever, it needs not a shell,
The octopus brain works ever so well.

Feeling and thinking with eight suckered arms,
No wonder this master of camouflage charms.

We once came to know one while surfing Oman,
When after days of squirting ink, it tried to hop on!

Common Octopus — Secret Spot, Oman

Puffer

The colorful puffer knew just what to do,
When snatched by an eel out hunting for food.

It couldn't escape with its tiny fins,
So, it puffed up its tummy and rough, spiky skin.

The eel had never, ever known such a scare,
And that poisonous taste – a sure sign to *BEWARE!*

The puffer was freed and to our disbelief,
It calmly returned to cruising the reef.

Porcupinefish — Okinawa, Japan

Quetzal

Far from the waves and sizzling black sand,
Is a dazzling bird, the bird of this land.

Its pretty songs echo through mountain mist,
And feathers flicker, when by the sun kissed.

Melody making high up in a tree,
Cloud forest quetzal – glorious and free.

Resplendent Quetzal — Chelemhá Cloud Forest, Guatemala

Rattlesnake

Whispering grasses and rustling leaves,
Send rattley shivers deep into me.

But the only rattler that the three of us spy,
Is one soakin' up rays beneath the hot Texas sky.

Western Diamondback Rattlesnake — Padre Island National Seashore, Texas

Scorpion

Mex 1 is a road, you'll want to explore,
As it snakes through the mountains and dry desert floor.

You'll see cacti and critters along the way,
Like a scorpion by the fire at Scorpion Bay.

Bark Scorpion — Scorpion Bay, Baja California, Mexico

Turtle

Big strong flippers steer her, above the seagrass bed,
After a trip guided by smells, and magnetics in her head.

Surfing currents for many weeks, with neither map, nor phone,
Back to lay her eggs in the sand, on the beach she knows as home.

Cruisy green sea turtle, with giant heart-shaped shell,
Living green on plants and algae, rider of current and swell.

Green Sea Turtle — Midigama Beach, Sri Lanka

Urchin

Sea urchins can see with their feet! Actually, they use them to sense light, but not shapes.

Can you sense light when your eyes are closed?

"Quit chomping kelp and poking our feet!"
Is all we hear from you soft-footed peeps.

While we busy urchins clear algae all day,
And keep *ab-a-lo-ne* hunters a nose-length away.

Cape Sea Urchin — Cape Peninsula, South Africa

Vaquita

Ten smiley vaquitas swim the Sea of Cortez,
With black-patched eyes on small rounded heads.

If you are lucky and sail past by chance,
You may spot a pair. Slow down! Take a glance.

But better than searching the sea where they roam,
Is working to save them at school and at home.

Vaquita Porpoise — Sea of Cortez, Mexico

Whale Shark

Could the biggest fish in our oceans be...
A whale of a shark, gentle and free?

That slurps in water and filters it slow,
For plankton and fish smaller than your toe.

So, if you're out surfing some tropical spot,
And see a van-sized fish with polka-dots...

Don't get too creeped and quickly paddle in
At first sight of a whale shark's five-foot-high fin!

Whale Shark — Indian Ocean, Mozambique

Xolo

Being hairless, these dogs can get sunburnt.

What is your best tip for staying safe in the sun?

A hairless Xolo (*sho-lo*) tames Puerto's huge tubes
Better than most surf dawgs at *Zi-ca-te-la* Beach do.

With no mane in her eyes or fur weighing her down,
She gets tubed before strutting her way back to town.

Xoloitzcuintli — Puerto Escondido, Mexico

Yellowfin

Some fish them for fun or know them from cans,
Or eat them on rice at poke bowl stands.

But listen up dude, yellowfin are cool!
They blast through warm seas and migrate in schools,

With other tuna, sharks, dolphins and rays,
All chasing their food, beneath the blue waves.

Yellowfin Tuna — Fernando de Noronha, Brazil

Zooplankton

Zooplankton drift freely in all seven seas,
From single-celled beings to tentacled jellies,

To tiny crustaceans like shrimp-shaped krill,
Zooplankton are the key to every fishy's fill.

So, while you may wow at whales and great whites,
Thank nature for planktons as you nod off tonight.

Zooplankton — Earth's Oceans, Lakes & Ponds

There's an art to life – living it!

"Exploring wouldn't be the same
without someone awesome to come
home to and trade stories with"

Grandma Pippa

Your turn to share:

*Draw a postcard of a
wild animal, however
big or small, that lives
in your neighborhood.*

*Send it to someone
you love!*

First printed and published in 2022 by Wiilder aps

www.wiilderworld.com
ISBN 978-87-94043-08-3

Published by Joachim Christgau
Co-written & Co-created by Joachim Christgau & Alex Whitman
Illustrations by Kristian Funder / Layout by Enrico Andreis

Printed in China. Paper in this book is certified by the Forest Stewardship Council. FSC promotes environmentally appropriate,socially beneficial, and economically viable management of the world's forests.

FSC
www.fsc.org
MIX
Paper from
responsible sources
FSC® C017606